THE VAUDEVILLE HORSE

THE VAUDEVILLE HORSE

ELIZABETH KERLIKOWSKE

Etchings Press • Indianapolis

This publication is made possible by funding provided by the Shaheen College of Arts and Sciences and the Department of English at the University of Indianapolis. Special thanks to the students who judged, edited, designed, and published this chapbook: Emma Knaack and Adam Lourenco Fernandes.

Published by Etchings Press
1400 E. Hanna Ave.
Indianapolis, Indiana 46227
All rights reserved

etchings.uindy.edu
www.uindy.edu/cas/english

Printed by IngramSpark

Published in the United States of America

ISBN 978-1-955521-09-3
26 25 24 23 22   1 2 3 4 5

Cover image courtesy of Ohio State University, Jerome Lawrence and Robert E. Lee Theatre Research Institute

Cover design by Emma Knack and Adam Lourenco Fernandes
Interior design by Adam Lourenco Fernandes

UNIVERSITY *of*
INDIANAPOLIS.

To my family for providing so much raw material:
I am indebted.

Table of Contents

DEPARTMENT OF THE INTERIOR

Poorly-lit Pure Michigan billboards encourage tourists to visit the mitten in their Land O Lincoln cars. FIPs we call them: fucking Illinois people. They have come for the ticks and poison ivy, for the poison sumac and mosquitos, to be swept off piers in Grand Haven or South Haven or St Joe. They have come for local candy on Mackinaw Island where we call them Fudgies. Morel hunters, mostly Hoosiers lost on hillsides, stumble onto our property in need of water and a ride back to the highway. The locals say men who look like morels find the most morels. A pint of whiskey at night; a quart of cream in the morning. The air sings with semis down-shifting, leaf blowers fall and spring, engine music of willful dumbasses just now vaccinated. Plump tourists love our lakes, weightless at last, but bloodsuckers love the lakes more and fleshy Ohio flesh. Income, we call them. We relax inside our obsessions: casinos, forests, ski resorts! Snowplows replace snow we just shoveled as they race by. Thank you! More exercise! Every weather burnishes its months, especially humidity, pollen and tornadoes. Welcome to a peninsula where speed limits are approximate, and we are just now comprehending roundabouts. Please don't signal.

FIVE STORIES THAT DO NOT PORTRAY ME IN THE BEST LIGHT

About depression, I mean, carrots.
He brought home multi-colored carrots and blue potatoes, a yellow pepper, salmon, wine. The paper bag kept throwing up delicacies, but it was too late. The thief had stolen his wife and left Niobe in her stead. "You don't have to cook the food," he said with exasperation; "you just have to eat it. "

About stinkbugs.
Stinkbugs like to dive into the pool of light fixture mounted to the ceiling. Attracted to the heat, unable to climb the smooth hill out, their bodies pile up like hard candy we're saving for later. I saw a stink bug throw himself from the lip of our lampshade into a proper woman's proper hair-do. I'd never seen her dance before. I'm telling you, it was funnier than kohlrabi.

About butter.
My son and I went to an Easter banquet at a Polish Hall. Leggy, beautiful girls waited table, my son pointed out, and the rest of the women were crones. Apparently women my age had been abducted. Strangers, we were seated at a crone table, one of whom carefully took the butter lamb, wrapped it in napkins and stowed it in her purse. The rolls were too dry to eat then, so my son stuffed them in his pocket. On the freeway, he threw them at cars that offended me.

About an earwig
The iron frying pan was over the flame before the earwig woke. When would the heat kill him? I could control that, towering over the stove, adjusting my science bifocals, increasing the fire power from 3 to 5. The earwig, all legs and ass pincers, ran now, shuffled, danced faster, fell twitching, twice. Too much. A paper towel wrapped him in his next life. I cooked my egg where he died.

About walnuts
They are in your cupboard like a bag of furry hearing aids. That is why you hardly ever touch them. But sometimes the recipe calls for walnuts, and you must finger their gnarled brains, petrified intestines, and with your ulu knife, smithereen them until they look like termite sawdust. You put the rest of the bag back for later, probably a year or two. Walnuts never expire. Enjoy that cookie.

GOODWILL AND THE RENAISSANCE

The ass was uncomfortable. Mary was tired. Jesus was fussy, and she thought it was because his halo didn't fit, pinching his aura.   "Joseph," she said, "We need to go to Goodwill and get new haloes."

"They sell them at Michael's, you know. That's closer."

Jesus was in full out wail now. "No. They're cheaper at Goodwill. They're 99 cents. At Michael's, they're $3.50. Plus they're closed on Sundays."

Joseph mulled. Two angels flew over. He thought about snatching a halo from the smaller one's head, but God seemed always to be watching.

Jesus fell asleep, finally, and they went to Goodwill: out of haloes, but they bought golden plates that floated behind their heads. She hadn't noticed the golden flecks in Jesus's eyes until they put them on.

Mary said, "That's so much better. No pinching. He's happy. Our boy likes a bargain."

HEADACHE

She was born with a steel helmet on. That's how she got to be old: the trunk falling from the rafters would have killed a normal child. She was just dazed for life. As a girl, she kept separate heads for each occasion where they would be most useful: her obedient head in the broom closet with the cleaning supplies and booze, her aquatic head under the raft where minnows swam through its hair, her clarinet head in the practice room where she made out with the tuba player. Her competitive head lived part-time in the basketball bin and part time with the globes and models of the solar system. At her first wedding, her dreamy head wore tiny braids. At the second, a mortar board. She kept domestic concentration in the weird metal flour drawer no one ever opens along with gifts for her husband. She maintained her seductive head in the nightstand and never combed its hair. Her road head was smashed into the glove compartment with driving gloves and hand sanitizer. She wore her mother head for so many years it wore out, but she was too tired to replace it. It was wrinkled and discolored, thin in spots, baggy in others, but having just one head was easier than maintaining all those others. When she was alone, she went headless, her face infant calm. You wouldn't recognize her.

HER PARENTS WERE A VAUDEVILLE HORSE

Their costumes lay around like pancakes of deflated elephants, trunks everywhere. She inherited and wore the four-limbed sweaters dragging the empty sleeves behind like a cootie's butt. It was hard to meet men. She tied the empty sleeves around her waist into a sort of obi, and that felt better. At art galleries and carnivals she searched for another freak who'd understand her yearning to be more than a horse, to be a couple. He came to her, a satyr in a velour shirt. No, just a man with empty arms waiting for her. They almost never left his shirt, it was that perfect. And it was striped like a zebra, which had way more prestige than a horse.

THE INTERNATIONAL SKIRT-MAKING COMPETITION

I heard about The International Skirt-Making Competition on the radio and knew I had to tell my daughter. I walked to Orcas Island and knocked on a stranger's door. When Rose answered, I could see she was already hard at work on her skirt, which hung from a utility belt and had large squares of burlap, canvas and red wool. There were deep pockets for holding everything a person might need. Her skirt was lined with pressboard; the individual panels were stitched together with razor wire, jute and staples. I was more concerned with flow, so my skirt was a space age fabric that moved like snow sifting off a roof. It snagged on everything and bunched like bugs in spider webs, which gave the material its texture. It caught every air current and then it was like time-lapse photography of fog moving over a lake. Angels were already phoning in their orders. When Rose put on my skirt, she felt beautiful. When I put on hers, I felt capable. It wasn't about the competition; yes it was.

JAGUAR XKE

"I can't see anything! I think I'm dead!" said the headlight.

"You're not dead. You're just burned out", said the parking light.

"Isn't that the same as death?"

The parking light had to be careful. She didn't want to scare the headlight. "Death is permanent; once you get a new bulb, you will still be a headlight."

"I will? This has never happened to me before."

"Oh, well, I've been replaced a couple times and I'm still me," she lied.

The headlight flickered. "Hey, I think I'm coming back!"

The parking light wanted to tell the headlight he would never come back and that tomorrow, there would be a new headlight and she would talk with it. "Headlight, I'll be with you tomorrow."

"Thanks," he said and meant it.

"Let me tell you a bedtime story."

THE LOGICAL THING

Something was irritating my gum, more than just the Lego-like shards of my teeth. Perhaps a sprinkle from recent ice cream had found a forever home. I excused myself—no, I didn't—I just started digging around in my mouth with my witch fingers until I found a new erratic. As I worked my tongue, sharp edges became apparent. My thumb and forefinger gave a yank, and painlessly, at least for me, a fossil dragonfly emerged. Beautiful and shiny with my spit. I must have swallowed it on a run up the dock to dive, mouth open, pushing off, taking that final gulp of air. I poured myself some whiskey—strictly as a disinfectant. As the dragonfly husk shivered in air for the first time in decades, its wings etched over with runes, serif and sans-serif. Certain this was a message, I found my magnifying glass but they were just designs drawn by breezes. My companions wanted to touch the dragonfly, but it was mine. I set it on the mantel for a few minutes, but it felt too exposed. My grandmother's jewelry box was too quiet and velvety. So I did the only logical thing: I swallowed the dragonfly but didn't chew—in case it wants to work its way out again.

MUSEUM OF BROKEN RELATIONSHIPS

Olinka Vištica watches couples on the carpeted dance floor, not easy to dance on carpet. One couple is simian yet gelatinous; the other, gnarled, maneuvering around mismanaged spines. Nonetheless, these couples both resemble her exlove and his new lady friend, handsome he and svelte her. Heartbreaking to see them everywhere, especially where they are not. In this year on this day she isn't the only one with a scotch-taped heart. What can be done for all the jilted lovers, for her friend who keeps old dreadlocks her ex braided, for the one whose marriage left her only with a series of license plates? She takes the box cutter from her purse (because in Zagreb it is always good to have boxcutters) and excises a six inch blue stripe from the flowered carpet, inches where all the dancers had placed a foot. The dancers don't notice, blinded by their exclusive loves. That blue stripe, under glass, becomes the first exhibit in the Museum of Broken Relationships.

IF MY GRANDFATHER WALKED TOWARD ME WITH TWO ARMS, I WOULDN'T RECOGNIZE HIM

My grandfather's arm was buried near Fife Lake on his brother Bill's farm. Bill was paid by the government not to grow anything, so he didn't. I never found the arm although I looked for it each visit. My grandparents weren't very good at burying things. I found my dog's grave shortly after they told me she'd run away. In our family, to put your elbow on the open window of a moving car was just tempting fate. Everyone knew what happened to Leo. At the farm the only thing to read was the Classic Comic book of *Moby Dick*. In the panels with the heaving ocean, the sea's ink was so black it was purple. The first few times I read it, I was fingerprinted. My great-grandparents lived across the road from the farm. They were tiny and poor. Grandma Dolly was the one who buried the arm. She was a spiritualist advisor. After the truck sheared off my grandfather's arm but barely tore his coat sleeve, after the bootleggers saved him and dropped him anonymously at the hospital, after everyone was notified—his parents, his wife with three young children— his mother drove three hours south to fetch the arm and bury it at the farm. Ahab stood on the storm-tossed deck, his ivory leg the brightest object on the page. It was hard to think of him as handicapped; he was so angry. When a one-armed man sits down at a piano, you don't expect much. My grandfather played by ear, and his hand flew over the keys as if it had wings; I swear I sometimes saw them. He could not tie his shoes. My grandmother knelt before him each morning. Double-knotted, so he would never have to ask for help. Grandma Dolly took my grandfather to her seances to prevent people from sticking a pin in her arm or worse, to test if she was really in a trance. My grandmother said when they lived at the farm after the accident, objects were always moving. My grandfather had a special knob on his steering wheel, required by law. It was not required that it be ruby red inside an ivory holder. Queequeg practiced a different kind of magic from Grandma Dolly, one that required more tattoos, which bled onto the newsprint. The farm people all believed in reincarnation. My mother died when my sister was born; ergo Ahab will be reincarnated as a whale. My grandfather told his mother he was having phantom pain. She went to the arm's grave and dug it up. Its fingers were clenched. She straightened them out, reburied the arm, and he was fine.

NATURAL HISTORY LESSON 26: PORCUPINES

The woman in the seat next to me had a porcupine on a leash.
Where I come from, I said, *we call those porkypines.* "Well, isn't that adorable." She got up and moved. I heard later he was her emotional support animal.

Whose porcupine is this? asked the maitre'd. *Its feathers are shedding on my ankles.*

We are mammals, whisper the porcupines in the dark they love. *We are not nasty rodents with little teeth who eat nothing but garbage. We eat fruit, leaves, Luxardo cherries, Twizzlers, Vegemite and kimchi when we can get it.*

Porcupines make quill baskets of their own quills, which regenerate. They sell them to Native Americans who sell them to tourists. This is called fair trade.

The 1896 Olympic tree-climbing team was nothing but porcupines from the Upper Midwest. Three Oles and a Sven.

I watched a porcupine spend the night eating termites from a garage door, upside down in the moonlight, which caught
the quills and made them look like a suit of sewing machine needles.

All porcupines are Aries with an occasional Taurus. Famous porcupines include Groucho Marx, Karl Marx, Mark Twain, Hal Holbrook, Walt Whitman, and Gertrude Stein.

They den in the hollows of trees, which they decorate with what's at hand. Some porcupines build walls of Wonder Bread. Some allow ailing birds to heal there. Most vote by absentee ballot. It's calmer for the other voters.

A balloon, a condom, and a porcupine walk into a bar.

ORIGAMI

By moonlight and from gum wrappers and doilies, the angel folds airplanes into star shapes, rings and meteors. In tiny golden script she writes the finders' names and cities then sprinkles cinnamon and anise on what pass for wings. Even an accidental encounter should smell good. Just before a storm she leaves her fleet on the picnic table for the wind's pick-up and delivery. The angel imagines her airplanes falling into a hand extended to receive a quarterback's pass or awaiting change at the store or perhaps a child holding out her first lost tooth. In the morning, the angel turns her face sunward for confirmation that her airplanes landed on the earmarked windowsills of those who needed a message from the universe or an angel or just wanted some kind of sign, even if it made no sense.

THE PEST

The mosquito looked at the dragonfly. "What is that you're doing?"

She was on her hands and brittle knees, her iridescent blue tail pointing toward the sun.

"This is the obelisk pose."

"I can do that," he said, but when he tried, he could only do crow pose. "I can make humans run from me!" he said. That was true, even if it was not from fear but annoyance.

"You are in the class called pests," she said. "Dragonflies belong to the class odonata, carnivorous insects with toothed mandibles."

"You are a pest," he retorted lamely. (She says I have class!)

"Au contraire, I am an obelisk." French was wasted on him, she quickly realized.

"Oh con trayer," he repeated. (So beautiful, so dragonfly!)

The sun disappeared. She lowered into plank to conserve heat. Being beautiful WAS a curse now that a mosquito had a crush on her. "Isn't it time for you to go bite people?"

"I'd rather stay here with you," he whined.

If she'd had a bib, she would have tied it on. "Come over here. I want to kiss you," she said.

(She loves me!)

After the mosquito, she was too full to return to obelisk. Besides, she could still hear him talking in there! What a pest!

PHYSICAL THERAPIST

On a scale of 1 to 10 how's the pain? Is it here? Does this involve it? You cup your
hand over it generally. Is it general pain? Can you hear it? Is that the spot? You're

wincing just relax. How's Rose? Is she in college now? We sent the twins to Gagie
school. Ok. I'm going to twist this. I'm applying pressure. Does it feel hot? Your

tolerance for pain is extremely high. The muscle narrows here and then wraps around
the joint. I don't know why that woman wraps her head in gauze. Bend, not your

good leg. Stop helping me. Just let it go. If you're in Chicago, see the Body Worlds
display. Actual human bodies injected with plastic, riding horses, maybe not your

cup of tea. Relax. But for me, better than cadaver class where organs are discolored by
the time we got them. This might feel cold. Uh-huh. Let's loosen the knot your

last injury tied. The horse is skinless; the musculature is clear. A man's running
without his skin. My daughter said he was running after his skin, a thought your

daughter might have. Let's switch to the ankle. Here? Here? Here? Ok. The synovial
fluid needs to be massaged back into the muscle. To strengthen this spot your

deformity has affected. Hip, ankle, knee, back. Cadaver class was in Marquette
last summer. It's the only way to see how things connect. Do ten squats. You're

quite strong considering. Can you balance on one leg? Put your back against the wall. Grasp. Flex. Release. Don't let me push it down. Push me away. You've got your

flexibility still. Good. Buy orthotics. Buy new shoes. Buy water shoes. Never be barefoot. You've got to build your quad. Biggest danger is a blood clot. You're

a good candidate for surgery. She drains the lymph glands. I don't know her well. The twins like science. So Rose will be a writer. Sit up. Nice day. I brought your

chart. Come next week on Monday, Tuesday and Wednesday. You'll do the pool two days. We can get you in shape for the surgery. Any questions? I'll jot your

times down on my business card, Elizabeth. Let me show you the brochure to Body Worlds. It's a little grisly. Look. Fruit flies around my lunch apricot! You're

free to go.

PRESERVATION WITH ORANGE PEEL

The orange tree holds its globes up to the porch light, also orange, in the charcoal night. Windows superimposed on the stucco that supports curtains of ivy. The primary limb reaches toward the tiny balcony stapled to the second floor. This is how the daughter escapes. The rope ladder invisible in daylight; cleats under mums a last resort for stealing in. Light wiggles in the attic: her mother's candle, late night writing. Blue light in the living room where her dad snores. She and her brother have built a fence of fingernails, scabs and teeth around the house to keep time from attacking their memories. Now they are adding oranges and rocks since their bodies have quit providing enough raw material. What's in the house gives her history, will, gumption, and some crazy. Even when its locked, it's open to her. There's a coal chute. Ghosts block doorways with their thin insistence on conversation. Grandpa talking about the circus again. Her uncle with the wild eye, politics. She peels the orange from her pocket. Volatile oils make apparitions disappear. *Is that you?* says her dad, rubbing his face the way he rubbed theirs with snowballs. "Just having an orange before bed." *Wish we still had that orange tree. Remember how it rubbed up against the house?* There was never an orange tree.

SEX LIFE OF THE DATE PALM

"The farmer's here," said the male blossom. "He's got the string."

The female blossom primped in a dew drop. "I know he's got to knot us together, but does he have to watch? Couldn't he look at the sunrise? His hands know the work."

"Sh. He's right here."

The farmer slipped several pollen-crusted stalks in the plump furrows. "It's the most meaningful part of my job," he thought.

"That's disgusting," hissed the female. "I can hear you!!"

The farmer thought, "I was only thinking it."

"Well, I heard it."

"Derek Jeter. Derek Jeter. Derek Jeter."

"What?"

"That works with my wife," he thought.

The male blossom was asleep, of course. "I'd complain to my mate here, but you know how pollination takes it out of him."

"I need some coffee," said the farmer. "Any for you?" But, having finished her cigarette, she turned to cultivating the date.

THE SHARK

Happy you are cranking out poems, cooking new dishes using produce from your garden, teaching, laughing, busy busy then you feel it coming like a hive after a new queen, a faraway train you feel before you see, the dark walk toward the principal's office, the shark music from Jaws at first just to frighten but then what makes the music wants to kill you, but wait, the shark wants you to do it yourself and it's full of suggestions: drive into that abutment, jump off the parking structure, slit your wrists and the shark suggests the best way is not across but parallel to the bone. The shark tells you you're ugly, stupid, untalented. It's amazing people can stand to look at you without retching. You smell the affliction on yourself. Your pilot light is low and now it's flickering and it flickers for days. You never cry; you can't stop crying. Your sunglasses don't protect you. And then something, some little something, happens. You drop a glass and it doesn't break or your bamboo grows an inch overnight or your cowlick is tamed and then maybe there is hope, there is a sliver of hope in your hand and it hurts but at least you can feel it, and being able to feel again means you're not quite dead, and there could be a thunderstorm with a power outage. That's wonderful because with candles and silence, the living room becomes a church and your husband is there to welcome you back, although he's been there all along. And you build a fire and watch it burn without wanting to jump in and the shark migrates to someone else's waters. The garden is calling and life begins again.

SOLSTICE 2020

Ice has brought down limbs and power lines. The city is quiet, at last, and dark. The man piles on coats and steps outside to marvel at stars thick as snowflakes. Though deer huddle near what was the garden, he walks toward them further from the house. The snow is nearly enough light. He's not sure if those are the deer or their shadows. His breath and their breath steams and disappears, inhaled by the cold. His neck aches from looking up at so many stars, stars always there but not often seen. He lies down in the snow and lets the sky be a star-studded blanket. Hooves crunch through ice. Warm and slick, a tongue slides over his face. The deer surround him, their breath like hot mushroom soup and wet dog. They nudge and prod him as they have always wanted. He is safer outside with them than inside with the virus. No traffic noise. He could be the only person left in the world. Stars, snow, deer: so simple. But cold, he struggles to his feet. The deer scatter back to the grove and his boots break the icy crust of this moment, the way it is when his feelings sometimes breach his body. His hand on the doorknob, he turns his back, still thick with icy snow, on the powerless world.

SUBURBAN GARNISH

At Thanksgiving, the man dragged from the basement the giant plastic bow and somehow hung it on the peak of the house. The house hated it, embarrassed by the cheap bow and lack of finesse with which the man attached it. Houses want to wear siding. They like to be decorated with woodpeckers. When snow falls, it should settle in shingles and dust the roof, but the bow turned it into sleet. And they spot-lit it. The house closed its eyes and tried to sleep through the holidays, but it knew the bow was there knocking on its skull when the wind blew. Across the street inflatable Santas and Elves lay in the yard by day like spent rubbers. In a March rain, the man would yank the bow down, leaving little scraps of it on the nails. The house didn't mind the scraps; it wasn't their fault.

TABLE MANNERS

The Periodic Table opens the restaurant door for the Multiplication Table to enter. *Table for two?* says the maitre d'. *Sorry.* Periodic Table can't see an empty seat, every chair filled by imposters! He pounds his francium corner on the picnic table, *"I'll tell you what's not a table, that table of contents right over there! The one whose page number is resting on the axle of the color wheel. It's not a table; it's a list!"* His helium and hydrogen edge closer to each other. He says loudly, "Tables of contents are blurring the distinction between honest-to-God tables and them. There is one Periodic Table. There are millions of tables of contents." He was frothing a little; sometimes unstable. Multiplication Table says, *"There's room to sit outside near the water table. C'mon."* Periodic Table turns and beholds the roulette wheel, red and black and lonely. The discussion of contents is tabled for now, but Periodic Table neither forgets nor forgives.

THANATOPHILIA

Since your unimpending death moved in with us, quarters are tight. You and she on the couch snuggled up under the pall, your nightly catalog of tv tragedies. You give her all your attention, wanting and not wanting her to tell you what you don't want to know. When I speak, she speaks louder. When I think I'm talking just to you and you don't answer, I know you're both crypt shopping. You snap at me because your patience only extends as far as death. She shares your bed and loves the syncopation of your apnea. She urges you to eat more, points out the dying are thin; that smoking is just not that bad and kind of sophisticated. She says you could exercise a lot less. That might bring the big one on. She's busted up our card playing by diverting your attention to the omnipresent question: heart attack or stroke? My money's on stroke. Until then, absolutely never stray in thought from your death. That's what keeps her alive.

TRIBUTE TO MARY HATCH

"I have a friend who's a painter, and when she's stuck for ideas, she squeezes another character into the scene," said Warming-Her-Hands-By-The-Fireplace.

"That's stupid," said Leaning-On-The-Mantel.

"If there was more scotch, we could all be having a good time." Looking-Pasty-At-The-Open-Bar closed her eyes and sighed.

"Chaos would ensue!" remarked That-Tuxedo-Has-Seen-Better-Days.

"Scotch chaos or character chaos?" asked Speaks-Under-Her-Breath.

Looking-Pasty-At-The-Open-Bar swooned. Her dress fluttered like a rise of butterflies on floral upholstery. Warming-Her-Backside wanted to know if dinner was served since she'd been turned around warming her hands. Lighting-A-Cigarette had admired her backside; her hair smelled like biscuits. Rain was gravel against the windows. The doorbell rang. Twa corgies skidded across the floor. Pink descended on a chandelier. Dinner was never served.

TURNING IN

"It's time," said the cold.
"No. It's too early. I'm not ready," said the lake.

The cold was much older than the lake and knew
that November was not too early but perfect.

"I want to see the winter I only feel. I want to know
how the hill looks clabbered with snow."

The cold sighed. White caps shivered on the lake.
"You're three seasons old. You're still putting on
shore. Now it's time to rest."

The lake said, "Well, I'm not going to rest. I'm going
to make mussels and grow trout three feet long and
return all the lost junk on my bottom to the rightful
owners. That will show you I'm ready for winter."

The cold said, "Perfect. That's exactly what a lake should
do in winter." The cold loved the lake's spunk.

The lake started crying.   "What's wrong?" asked the cold.
"There's something in my eye!"
                    "That's ice, you baby."

UTILITY DRAWER

Said the pen to the paintbrush and crochet hook, "It's like we're sister-wives. That hand just keeps us here in the drawer, waiting for its next whim."

The paintbrush said, "I think of it as a time of germination."

The crochet hook said, "I get motion sickness sometimes anyway."

The pen said, "You both think too much. We are tools; that's all."

"No!" the paintbrush objected. "I am an artist."

"Moi aussi!" said the crochet hook.

"No. You are a craftsperson," said the pen to the hook. "Everyone knows that."

The crochet hook looked down her nose at the pen. "Oh, you mean useful?"

The pen turned over and nodded off with the Number 2s.

"He is so cynical," said the crochet hook.

"Don't be hard on him. He has no memories," the paintbrush explained. "My bristles lived on a pig. I still feel the sun on me. Do you remember before you were a crochet hook?"

"I was thinking the other day: I loved being ore, so snug. And smelting, though hot, felt good. I never dreamed I'd have such a sleek shape; I'm pretty happy."

"It's not like that for the pen. He was born plastic; that's all he is. Ink flows through him, the hand guides him, all he knows is what he's been forced to write."

The crochet hook almost felt bad for the pen, but then he woke up and starting kicking the drawer to get the hand's attention. The drawer opened, the hand reached in, grabbed the pen and hurled it into the wastebasket, where it continued fussing.

The drawer shut. After a while, the paintbrush said, "It's kind of nice with him gone."

"It is," said the hook. She hesitated, "I am an artist, too, aren't I?"

"Of course you are," said the paintbrush, because she knew how to make something what it wasn't.

WHEN BUYING A HOME, ALWAYS ASK TO SEE THE MAP OF ABANDONED DREAMS.

Note the incomplete French Drain which became Le Great Tarpaper Bay, highlighted in winter by the Visqueen Memorial Bundle. The owner's ladder, Death Wish, rests against the gutters he douched with the hose. Near the Door No One Ever Opens by the inviting Bench No One Ever Sits On, Mulch Berms never release their goodness knowing they'll be replaced before they can compete their work. Arid Bird Bath complements Big Tree with Ghost of Tree House No One Ever Played In. Twig X-ings litter the yard and can drive a person crazy. Here is What The Streetsweeper Missed and the music of Cement Strummed With A Rake. Two Attempts at Landscape gasp in the front yard. Invisible sign that reads: No sticks. Dead leaves not welcome. Driving On Wrong Side Of Street Zone along property to mailbox. In the back, Washed Rock Basin, bathed by hand twice yearly. A Peripatetic Labyrinth spanning three backyards the owner follows on his quest for entries in the Pine Cone Derby, filling The Ancestral Yard Waste Bag with infinite cones from Maimed Trees to allow more sun on Le Great Tarpaper Bay. Mystery Zone we believe contains a Patio with Unused Grill and Lawn Furniture Covered With Plastic, Half-Inflated Pool for the Grandkids That Never Visit.

BIRDS IN THE 21ST CENTURY

They were not necessary. We regarded them as we did sequins on a sweater or the movement of rickrack around a hem. Birds were doodles in the margins of our pages. They were not essential like air and water, but they filled the trees with music, added color to winter and amazed us with their tiny powers of flight. They were always busy pulling worms from the ground, sleeping with one eye open while balancing on a wire. You try it. Their motley nests in ivy, in corners, in trees, on the ground hid them from us and smaller predators. Their eggs wore the tartans of different country sides or opted for sky blue, but birds stopped being necessary when we moved inside. Once we read the weather in their migrations, but now there's tv. Sometimes a warbler thumped into a window and dropped stunned or worse. Children buried them with beloved pets; some birds weighed less than a penny. The birds needed to hear each other sing so they stayed up later, rose earlier because of human din. Illumination everywhere all the time wore them out. No one found long jewels of blue jay feathers in the grass. Bird baths grew moss with no visitors. Bugs thrived without birds, even less reason to go outside. Birds were the new unicorns of bedtime stories. People who remembered them were asked again and again to describe how ducks landed feet first on a pond, how hawks snatched sparrows from the air, how, with a great deal of fluttering, the cardinal mates landed on the windowsill to feed each other seeds, and about the wren who lined her nest with rabbit fur. Unbelievable that such small, inventive creatures so unlike us lived in our lifetime, magicians of the air, sign of spring, what I hang around my neck in shame.

THE WORRIED UMBRELLA

The woman carried the umbrella away from the ocean.

The umbrella said," I can still see the other umbrella we left behind."
The woman said, "Don't worry. It will always be there."

"It's fading," said the worried umbrella.
"But you can still see it, can't you?"

"Yes, but only its bones."
"Well," said the woman, "those are the last to go."

"Will I be able to see it in the dark?"
"Can you see in the dark?"

"No."
"Then no, but in the morning, it will still be there…a little. You will never forget it. These flowers we're walking through, the old people called them flags. When I see them, I see the old people."

"I can't see it!" gasped the umbrella.
"Yes you can. It's right over my left shoulder."

"Ok. Maybe I can make it out."

WHAT SHE DOESN'T WRITE

She wants her poem to be a wand bedazzling trees with dew drops and fireflies, subtle and thought-provoking. Instead her poem runs barefoot to the compost and likes the mudfeel squishing between its toes. The poems she didn't write meet for wine and repartee in a darkened corner of The Park Club tea room. They are all thin and admire that about each other. Her poems intend to square dance at Bell's but instead just drink and tell embarrassing stories about themselves. They laugh hard and one of them farts. The poem in her mind is a broken mirror put back together so that only the fine lines of the shattering show. On the page, it's a stack of wet boots melting on the kitchen floor. Any refinement is white sugar, sweet but finally not satisfying. She thinks she wants her poem to reside in the New Yorker, but in the dark, it sneaks out with spray paint to tag City Hall.

SMOKING DOKE IN THE DINDIN WITH YOU

Table of contents

ACKNOWLEDGEMENTS

Peninsula Poets: "Her Parents Were a Vaudeville Horse"

KYSO Flash: "Museum of Broken Relationships", "The Inter national Skirt-Making Competition", "At Tabor Hill", "The Logical Thing", "Tribute to Mary Hatch"

Calyx: "Preservation with Orange Peel"

Barstow and Grand: "Natural History Lesson 26: Porcupines"

sleet: "When Buying a Home, Ask to See the Map of Abandoned Dreams"

MacQueen's Quinterly: "Goodwill and the Renaissance", "If My Grandfather Walked Toward Me with Two Arms I Wouldn't Recognize Him"

COLOPHON

Typeset in Volkorn, Rosewood Std and the occassional Altesse Std

ABOUT ETCHINGS PRESS

Etchings Press is a student-run publisher at the University of Indianapolis that runs a post-publication award—the Whirling Prize—as well as an annual publication contest for one poetry chapbook, one prose chapbook, and one novella. On occasion, Etchings Press publishes new chapbooks from previous winners. For more information about these contests and the Whirling Prize post-publication award, please visit etchings.uindy.edu.

Previous winners and publications:

Poetry
2022: *A Place That Knows You* by Tiwaladeoluwa Adekunle
2022: *The Vaudeville Horse* by Elizabeth Kerlikowske
2021: *My Mother's Ghost Scrubs the Floor at 2 a.m.* by Robert Okaji
2020: *Vaginas Need Air* by Tori Grant Welhouse
2019: *As Lovers Always Do* by Marne Wilson
2018: *In the Herald of Improbable Misfortunes* by Robert Campbell
2017: *Uncle Harold's Maxwell House Haggadah* by Danny Caine
2016: *Some Animals* by Kelli Allen
2015: *Velocity of Slugs* by Joey Connelly
2014: *Action at a Distance* by Christopher Petruccelli

Prose
2022: *Triple Point* by Laura Story Johnson (essays)

2021: *Bad Man Love Stories* by Curtis VanDonkelaar (fiction)

2020: *Three in the Morning and You Don't Smoke Anymore* by Peter J. Stavros (fiction)

2019: *Dissenting Opinion from the Committee for the Beatitudes* by Marc J. Sheehan (fiction)

2018: *The Forsaken* by Chad V. Broughman (fiction)

2017: *Unravelings* by Sarah Cheshire (memoir)

2016: *Pathetic* by Shannon McLeod (essays)

2015: *Ologies* by Chelsea Biondolillo (essays)

2014: *Static: Stories* by Frederick Pelzer (fiction)

Novella

2022: *Goodbye to the Ocean* by Susan L. Lin

2021: *Miss Alma May Learns to Fight* by Stuart Rose

2020: *Under Black Leaves* by Doug Ramspeck

2019: *Savonne, Not Vonny* by Robin Lee Lovelace

2018: *Edge of the Known Bus Line* by James R. Gapinski

2017: *The Denialist's Almanac of American Plague and Pestilence* by Christopher Mohar

2016: *Followers* by Adam Fleming Petty

Chapbooks from Previous Winners

2022: *slighted.* by Chad V. Broughman (fiction)

2020: *Fruit Rot* by James R. Gapinski (fiction)

2016: *#LOVESONG* by Chelsea Biondolillo (microessays with photos and found text)

ELIZABETH KERLIKOWSKE is a Michigan native, reflected in her speech, outlook, and general friendly demeanor. She is the author of numerous chapbooks, including *Last Hula* and *Rib*, the full-length books *The Shape of Dad*, *Dominant Hand*, and *Art Speaks*, an ekphrastic book with painter Mary Hatch. She was awarded the Kalamazoo Community Medal for the Arts in 2017 for her work with Friends of Poetry and the Poetry Society of Michigan.